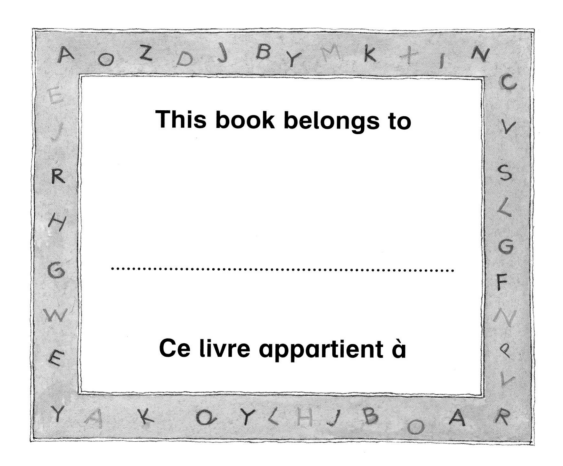

This book belongs to

....

Ce livre appartient à

D1493032

To parents and teachers

We hope this book will be fun to use in either English or French. Here are a few helpful tips:

- When you start a foreign language, it's comforting and very useful to learn words which are similar to your own language, like the words in this book.

- Although the words and letters look very similar in French and English, they are not usually *spoken* the same way. Have fun pronouncing the foreign language together. Use the pronunciation guide if necessary.

- Don't worry if your pronunciation isn't absolutely correct. The pronunciation guide will help but it cannot be completely accurate. You should read it as naturally as possible, but don't roll the r. Put stress on the letters in *italics* e.g. lombool-*onss*. Move on as soon as possible to speaking the words without the guide. Ask a French person to help you if you can.

- Encourage the children to have a go and give lots of praise. Little children are usually quite unselfconscious and this is excellent for building up confidence in a foreign language.

- Use the full alphabet at the top of the page to learn the alphabetical order. Try saying the whole alphabet in English and French and answer the quiz questions at the end of the book.

- Finally, use the beautiful frieze as a talking point: the children can pick out objects they know in French and perhaps learn new words too. They can also make up stories about the little characters and the exotic locations.

This edition first published 2008 by b small publishing ltd., The Book Shed, 36 Leyborne Park, Kew, Richmond, Surrey, TW9 3HA, UK
www.bsmall.co.uk
ISBN-13: 978-1-905710-48-5   All rights reserved.   © b small publishing ltd., 1994 & 2008   5 4 3 2 1
French Claudine Bharadia & Marie-Thérèse Bougard   *Editorial* Catherine Bruzzone and Susan Martineau
Design Lone Morton & Scott Gibson   *Production* Madeleine Ehm
Colour Reproduction Vimnice Printing Press Co. Ltd.   *Printed in China* by WKT Company Ltd.

Alphabet

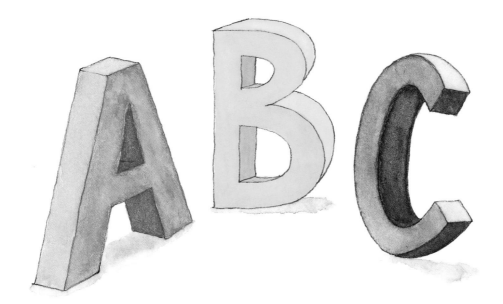

L'alphabet

lalfabeh

Catherine Bruzzone

Illustrations by Louise Comfort
Ilustré par Louise Comfort

b small publishing
www.bsmall.co.uk

a b c d e f g h i j k l m

Aa

ambulance
l'ambulance

ah

lombool-*onss*

n o p q r s t u v w x y z

Bb ball
la balle

beh   lah bal

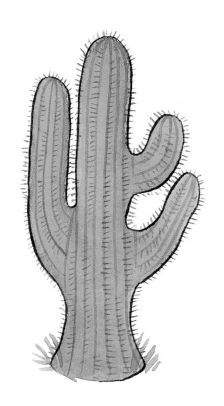

Cc

cactus
le cactus

seh

ler kak-*toos*

Dd **dolphin**
le dauphin

deh   ler doh-*fah*

a b c d e f g h i j k l m

Ee **elephant**
l'éléphant

er   lellay-*foh*

Ff fire
le feu

eff   ler fer

a b c d e f g h i j k l m

Gg gorilla
le gorille

shay   ler gor-*ee*

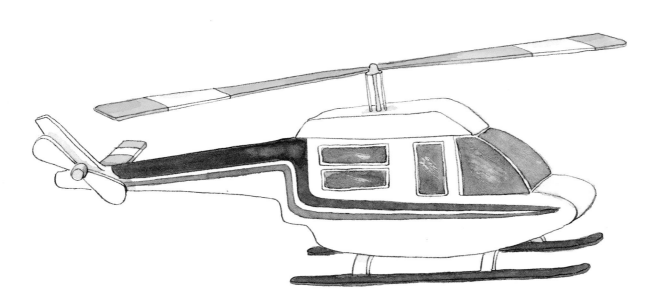

Hh

helicopter

l'hélicoptère

ash

lellicop-tair

a b c d e f g h i j k l m

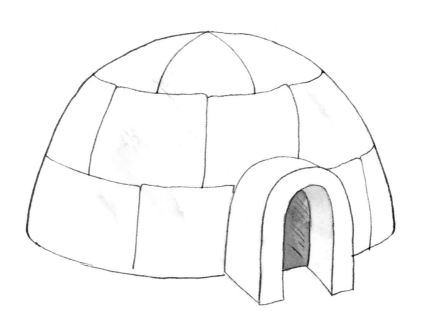

Ii igloo
l'igloo

ee   lig-*loo*

Jj jungle
la jungle

shee   lah shun-gl'

a b c d e f g h i j k l m

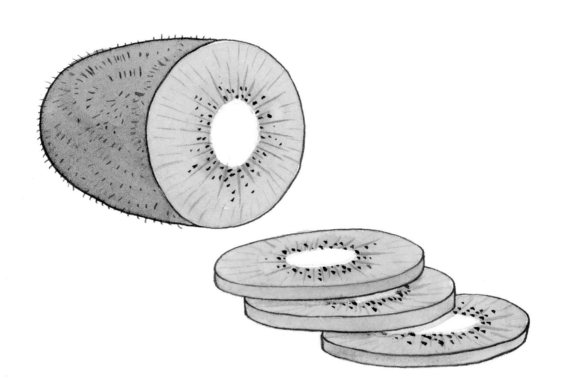

Kk kiwi
le kiwi

kah   ler kee-*wee*

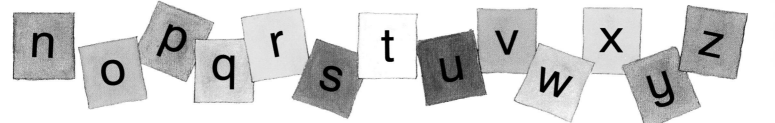

n o p q r s t u v w x y z

Ll lion
le lion

ell   ler lee-*yoh*

a b c d e f g h i j k l m

Mm

mountain
la montagne

em

lah mon-*tyne*

n o p q r s t u v w x y z

Nn night
la nuit

en lah nwee

Oo ogre
l'ogre

o'   loh-gr'

n o p q r s t u v w x y z

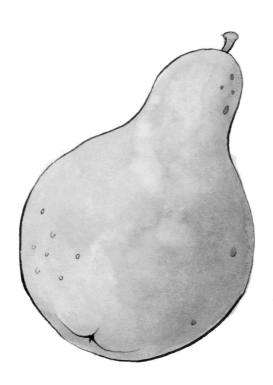

Pp pear
la poire

peh   lah pwah

a b c d e f g h i j k l m

Qq quintuplets
les quintuplées

koo

leh kan-too-*pleh*

Rr reindeer
le renne

air   ler ren

a b c d e f g h i j k l m

Ss

sun
le soleil

ess

ler sol-*ay*

n o p q r s t u v w x y z

Tt **tomato**
la tomate

teh   lah toh-*mat*

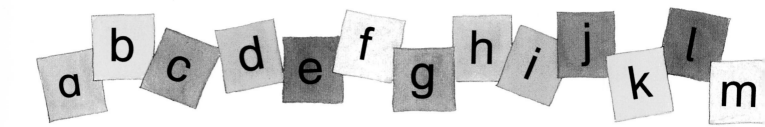

Uu universe
l'univers

oo   loony-*vair*

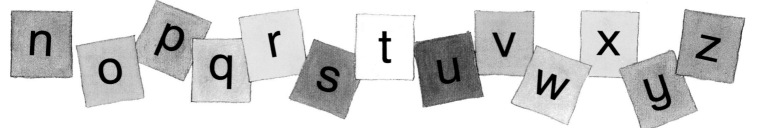

Vv

violin
le violon

veh

ler vee-o-*loh*

a b c d e f g h i j k l m

Ww

wok
le wok

doubl' *veh*   ler wok

n o p q r s t u v w x y z

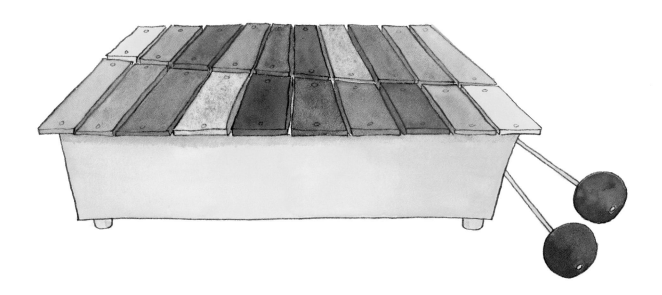

Xx xylophone
le xylophone

eeks

ler kseelo-*fon*

a b c d e f g h i j k l m

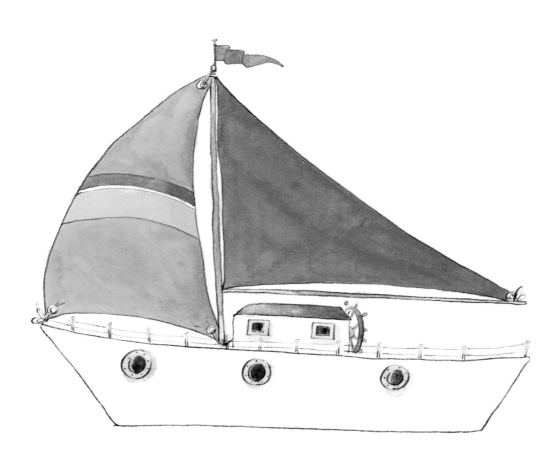

Yy **yacht**
le yacht

ee-grek   ler yot

Zz

zoo

le zoo

zed ler zooh

The End

Fin

fah

ABC QUIZ

Read these aloud in French, in the **correct** alphabetical order.

 la **b**alle

 l'**h**élicoptère

 l'**a**mbulance

 l'**i**gloo

 le **c**actus

 le **g**orille

Can you say the names for the following pictures in French?
Now say them in alphabetical order.

j

v

d

l

s

n

p

m

t

b   c   d   e   g   i   k   m

What are the missing letters?
Say them out loud in French. Now say the whole alphabet.

n   o   s   t   u   w   y   z

Check the answers by looking back through the book.

Other titles in this series:

ISBN: 978-1-905710-49-2

ISBN: 978-1-905710-47-8

b small publishing

If you have enjoyed this book, look out for our
other language learning books for children.
Order them from any good bookshop or request a catalogue from:
b small publishing ltd.
The Book Shed, 36 Leyborne Park, Kew, Surrey, TW9 3HA, UK
email: books@bsmall.co.uk
website: www.bsmall.co.uk